RIDDLE

RIDDLE

Diane Furtney

HEADMISTRESS PRESS

ISBN-13: 978-0998761077
ISBN-10: 0998761079

Cover art © 2015 Terry Castle, "Dyke Drama"

Cover & book design by Mary Meriam
Text in Adobe Garamond Pro, titles in Essonnes

PUBLISHER
Headmistress Press
60 Shipview Lane
Sequim, WA 98382
Telephone: 917-428-8312
Email: headmistresspress@gmail.com
Website: headmistresspress.blogspot.com

To J. M.

Contents

I. Before Twenty-One

Riddle   1
Logic at 14   3
Logic at 17   4

II. Mexico, San Francisco, New England

Mexican Morning   9
Sometimes in One's Twenties   13
The Only Thing   15
She Was   18

III. Something You Make Me Think Of

Jeredith   23
Forsythia intermedia   27
What to Wear   30
Friends in Middle Age   32
This One   35
Sailing to Mytilene   37

Notes   45
Acknowledgments   47

I. Before Twenty-One

Riddle

I am the oddity that is un-strange.
I'm the silver that rhymes with orange.

I am the slow,
obstinate plant that grows

at the rate of sediments
and infloresces extravagantly about once

a decade. To the sphinx,
my question made for raised wings,

squawks, and flight
into a bedroom mirror, in the light

of which was another face, another
woman, whose rhyme of course we need not further

search for. Her wavering look: enraged,
triste, and disengaged.

That her silver and orange but subfusc
longings could not be entirely masked

by her marriage and her dire pretenses,
I am the living evidence.

Justice, then, I'm a form of,
because I'm the shove

of hidden desire into egregious shape,
the moon's dark side that rotates

into view. I am the glare
of Is rather than the glare

of Seems, a minor-key
and irritating line of melody

following a two-generational family lie
that was cacophony. Who am I?

Logic at 14

Tulsa, late 1950s

The answer is not in childhood's
information. It's in weird social amplitudes

and constrictions that have to be decoded,
including hallway hatreds,

wrong and un-wrong outfits, jokes.
It might be somewhere in books.

It's in jobs, maybe, later, where
more people could be studied. It has to do with stares

from drivers when you step in front
of cars and, slowly, confront

the feelings about stepping
back—and with slumber-party "smooching"

by girls who "practice" on your still
face as if you were a fake, a doll.

It might connect with petty
thefts at stores—those moments of free-

gesturing throwaway. What
it will have to answer is not

the extra questions of lust
or love or What's it for? Just,

once and for all, Why
not die?

Logic at 17

Tulsa, early 1960s

There is this
world. Which, they say, is

assembled tightly:
women unite with men, A with Z.

No A-B or M-X combinations
can last, not in the congregations

of love. But that was the history, if true,
of the world up to now. I'm new,

and there might be, somewhere, a chorus
of new people, everything more porous

than what anyone admits or knows. Whole
groups might be acting freshly on what they feel

and anyone might approach anyone:
meet somehow and talk and then

go off into a laugh or a kiss
or a life—because the world is

hard but not just hard,
not just concrete slabs on the heart.

The world is also soft: it has to be
to make sense. It's the ice-green of baby

lichen on limestone stacked like log-wood
by a pool—ninebark and dogwood

on the bank; a turtle noses up in the watercress
and sunfish make C's and S's

between the stems; in the old beech
woods, there are dots of light on the deeps

of fallen leaves. The world is . . .
It's there and huge, and it's . . .

II. Mexico, San Francisco, New England

Mexican Morning

Puerto Vallarta, 1970

Chirps and grunts from the spined
shrubs have been close behind

the wooden shutters since dawn,
a hot dawn. Those sounds go on

all day—slow repeats,
and like shifting pieces of heat,

here at my temporary, overgrown
house: two weeks in a yellow town,

a village really, triangular and wedged
from the sea to the climbing edge

of jungle woods. Here where you pick
a desire, any desire . . . If I walk

out and around to the *cocina*
leaning against the house, heating the casino's

breakfast and my own,
if I stand behind the young woman

who, this time, has paused
at an angle over the heated stones as

I whisper, "I know you are not
from this village" and, "Never mind the cart

in the distance creaking its blue wheels,
the orange dog behind it, the field

of jacaranda matted down the fence,
the corn-stone steps,

dust on each edge,
all the stacked cubes of the village". . .

—or if the shells dangling
from red and blue threads hanging

at the window slats make a tiny
susurration, and a shiny

centipede shuffles like a clever
vegetable farther

along the roughwood shelf four
inches above the floor,

then the bright design
in or out of the room this time

has only shifted at its edges like
pieces in a kaleidoscope . . . If I

draw my fingernail down
her arm, shoulder to elbow, one

time only, if I lick her nape,
and time in the gaps

of that design has all
but solidified, and on this same hill

another woman, across yellow cans,
calls her knobby produce for sale and a man's

deep voice drops like a stone
from high up the *barranca* and is gone . . .

—if instead I toss back the sheet
and the gauzy net,

if I swing my feet
down to the woven mat

and she has come and gone
from this brown and orange room again,

then another bright fragment
has shifted for a moment

along the wedge of the morning.
I have been inside this mobile design

for a week. With its quick or slow turns,
I might not even turn

now when a faint scraping
along the window clay or a scuffing

near the door does not disguise the fact
that she can make an imperfect

noise when leaving.
She'll be back: in the vending streets, in the heaving,

desultory waves, in the shouts, the pause
between calls, in the black haze

of the disco after midnight.
She will be back, for long or not,

before the straight noon rains
or the bellbird's afternoon clang, again

and again before the grunts
of another sun

—here where every mood is a woman,
every morning a woman,

here where
the jungle is constantly satisfied desire

and a constant shove
of more desire, and the mind moves and moves.

Sometimes in One's Twenties

San Francisco, 1970

Coasting out into the open
night: no requirements, no plan,

you're limber and vivid as darkness, and
your shoes, new, patterned with tan,

aren't scraping your skin,
you're ready, no attention,

no adjustments, are needed, it's end-to-end
lightweight. Not hard to imagine,

though not something you'd mention:
the Background Music of everything, unbroken,

is almost audible. Fervent
and velvet, the wind, and there's more than

enough of everything for everyone. Even
love might be about to pause in its motion

with a simple turn in your direction.
Of course, nothing has to happen

tonight: you're young, the nights extend
into every distance with no end . . .

But at a six-streeted corner all of a sudden
an invisible bird tweets; call it a wren,

purple-checked, newly arrived from the Garden
District of the moon; and

there's this fit of mind to body as the body bends
to the world, surely something also bends

this way in the commotion,
is about to encircle . . . portends . . .

The Only Thing

San Francisco, 1971
For S. B.

One a.m., and from the center
of the bed I looked at her

standing, watching me. Cross-legged
on the sheets, I was dogged,

calm, comfortable. The Cointreau
and our shared glass she set on the bureau,

then stepped, naked, to the middle
of the rug—her small

feet wide apart in the white
room's bluish darkness. Light

from three windows, side by side, prostrated
their rectangles toward her. —This is dated,

oh, forty years ago, forty-five?,
and from the center now of

a different life. There was a moment
while she decided, her eyes intent

in the simple dark: affectionate,
testing? Then she became the delicate

and sure representative
of the beautiful curve

at the center of a cube: reaching up,
she touched the ends of her fingertips,

tilted her head and shoulders back,
dropped her arms, and slid her hands down the back

of her thighs. When she reached,
flat-palmed, for the floor, each

foot angled outward to brace
her inverted crouch. The dark, long lace

of her hair kept spilling into the dark
between her arms as she pushed up into the arc

of a backbend wheel, and held. One
of the strips of window light led on,

like a road, beneath her spine.
On its chain—a hesitant, wavering line—

a small gold disc moved slowly
up her throat. It was oddly

without boundary or mess, that night
—our only night, as it turned out—

without plights or pretense.
There was pep, there was a sense

of speed and pause as
what was described was the locus

of points surrounding the surround:
equidistancings on new ground

and scrambles at the center of everything.
It feels like knowledge of the only thing

worth knowing: endlessness. Being caught
and being freed. I will not say that it is not.

She Was

San Francisco and Massachusetts, mid-1970s

She was someone who delimits events
in the future, or a few of them. For instance,

I doubt that any threat or urgency
—though I'd be in tears—could bring me

to a phone to search for her. She was
the one who, for years after, because

life without her dark and smooth addition to it
could not be thought about,

I allowed, or did not disallow,
racket and mess and a small crowd

of affairs having peculiar
geometries, the more impossible the better

—as a diversion,
I suppose, an exchange: fresh pain

for old, pain like a lamp, and to be rubbed.
No doubt that big-clubbed

suffering over her
was itself diversion from something earlier

and familial—like everyone else's.
And *that* loss

diverts your sense
from some more general pain about existence?

She was the one for whom I walked
the night floors, wish-ridden, choked,

weeping, violent.
Of course, she became a moment

in the division of knowledge,
mind from body. If we stood on a ledge

at night, I used to think, or in the corners
of a silent stadium—no markers,

in blackness—my body could, I knew, step straight
to hers without a word or thought,

as the shortest distance between
two points. She was, then,

the demolishment—necessary?—
of the determined wish I still carried,

to live as something perfect,
never to intersect

with the dull,
inert, slack-mandibled

thuggishness of life lived as cliché
—including the cliché that a "weak" woman may

just be using her powers in another way,
or the cliché that when you've been betrayed,

you find your friends all knew. Earlier,
she was a disaster that—like most disasters?—

had been chosen, sort of. There was
a moment on a west-coast city bus

when I looked at her looking at her double
in the window, saw the face and face of trouble,

and knew I could and might and would adore her,
though I didn't completely like her, or

not much. I think one day I claimed
—whispered, murmured—that the bases of my DNA

had altered to spell the letters of her name,
to make "new proteins." Probably. Time

proliferates things like that: etiolates
memories, elongates

and twists them in a crowded space.
She was a past that has branched and twigged. Trace

with your right hand the right-hand wall
of a maze—say, a leafy wall—and that will

lead you out; or rather, will deliver
you to the gap in the topiary where,

just past a flagstone step
in the opening shrubbery, drops

the abyss.
She was that leafy wall, more or less.

She was the lush, absurd gamble
—after which, for five years or so, you self-reassemble.

III.   Something You Make Me Think Of

Jeredith

Columbus, Ohio, 2001

1.

On a pressed-back chair pulled close
to our trestle table, the one we chose

for the acorns carved in its supports,
she sits—in turquoise blouse, red shorts—

and reads in our quiet, white
dining room under wood-slatted light,

her legs crossed and one bare
foot tapping the air.

It could be fourteen years ago
in Berkeley, in her white-walled studio,

it could be an example-scene
showing the sum of tiny changes that mean,

eventually, large change. She was in grad-student
jeans then, the chair wicker, the sun aslant

through a beige blind, falling through
a glass-topped table to glisten on new,

red toenail polish, her right foot
tapping the air to that same beat,

which I think I might have briefly
heard a time or two, maybe.

Is she, or is she not,
the rock of my life? Is any woman that?

The past is a rock, or almost. The sense
of uselessness condenses,

from about mid-childhood, into almost-rock.
Boredom and its anger are a rock,

almost. But she takes her time.
Her displacing erosions take their time.

She is a rise and fall in sea level
that tilts a slab of sediment. She's small-

grained sand, abrading, through the air.
She's low-pressure, counterclockwise weather.

2.

Teasing, I said
to the back of her head:

"Why any two people take up together
and define the other

as a need, is not as hard to understand,
considering the hand-in-hand,

paper-doll nature of first desire,
as why it is that certain lovers do not tire."

She rolled to face me, bent her arm
to prop her head, and smiled: the sum

of oddity, she who was happy
in a marriage and could marry happily

again. How is it she can recognize
so much, including evil in its tiny, pale disguises,

but the knowledge does not alter
her kindness? She has sophistication without the falter,

without the embitterment that hits like a wind,
sharp and reasonable, when you turn a corner. Send

for that everywhere, look high and low.
Minute to minute how she exists, I don't know

and I would like to know. She's apples
and oranges? She's an inclined plane that rattles

as it rolls a ball to spring
a switch that rings a bell that swings

to light a flame? That's how she works? No,
probably not: the Rube Goldberg gizmos

of the heart sooner or later
over-heap and totter

and by now would have collapsed.
"Are you partitioned?" I've asked her. "Apsed?

Do you experience A through L, for instance,
in some spacious section of your mind, then advance

to another, larger room?"
What is she up to? We are as doomed

as any others, of course. Time has not
altered its nature on our account.

It uses her and me as it uses you, to express,
not always interestingly, its fields of stress,

including days attenuated or over-dense.
But who wouldn't stay with her? She makes no sense.

Forsythia intermedia

For Jeredith, on anniversary 18

Yellow for a week, so yellow
it could be a sound from a bellows

only a hound—an exuberant hound
of the Eocene—could hear. Around

humans, it's begun
to develop an ability to grin

in a kind of vegetable
hysteria, all the arms mobile,

about to get up ("I'm yellow!")
and run around the yard. And so

it's the wavelength, mid-yellow,
of our two days in Tahoe

and, later, hours on the winter beaches
of the California coast, plus luteous

mornings and xanthic afternoons
on road trips across the craton

of Ohio. Of course, there are also
those canes to consider, scabby-yellow,

their lenticels resembling impetigo.
Silhouetted on grubby snow,

they're a mess, a recalcitrant mass
—like, for us, the arching dread of illness

and some other life-events:
that ogress landlady in Columbus, for instance,

Transylvanian German, seventy-eight,
who tore up live-robin nests on our slate

front porch and had our full-grown,
backyard maple tree cut down

because "Dey make a mess, de leafs"
—but really because she could make us stand in grief,

weeping in the yard for love of that tree,
while her timorous and secret and angry

desire for each of us finally
settled at the level of her envy.

They were November-yellow,
those leaves, as wide as hands. Below

them all, our *intermedia* along the fence
had leaves of just three inches, with no-nonsense

margins to halfway down the blades
and tiny zigzags toward the tips: unfaded

evidence that it can be the interval
after flowering that's reliably beautiful

in close-up: repeating errands,
house adjustments, plans,

invoices, lists,
baseboard dust dispensed with

—various tiny greeneries
headed toward some yellow anniversary.

What to Wear

It's your posture,
it's the way you don't think to make overtures

to the male personnel,
it's the way your conversation omits marital

dilemmas A, K, and P through T.
But what it eventually

means is, you haven't got a thing
to wear. You could girl it up, you could fling

about in a dress every minute,
it could be cerise taffeta, you could bat

your eyes like ruffles and smile like rickrack,
but it would still take

only one week for an office
of fifty people to deduce

what everyone out to the farthest edges
of your family managed to dredge

into semi-awareness by the time
you'd entered the peculiarity realm

of first grade. And yet,
nevertheless: your outfit

could be green and yellow on Thursdays,
you could spell out the facts during every

telephone transaction
("'G' as in 'Grateful;' 'A' as in

'Attitude;' 'Y'
as in 'Yippee-ki-yay'"); you could identify

yourself and your partner
with a pointing, public finger

"This is the woman
—I also am a woman—

with whom I've lived—in the sense
of 'living intimately with'—since

the birth of time, to whom I've
been faithful, who has overgrown my life

like moss, who graces my every hour,
and whom I love.") Even then, your

draped ensemble would still be
the swingline cloak of invisibility

with grommeted, tie-front hood
whenever you provoke another brood

of doubts ("You're *really* gay?") if you so much
as snap on a necklace. The Crutch

Store of cliché is where they need for you
to shop. Where's the inventive retailer who

could do us all some good, who has no bins
of orange, pilled, eight-button cardigans?

Friends in Middle Age

For M. T., in Ohio

Better behavior from me, overall
(prodded by the wherewithal

of gratitude, which punishment
by the usual authorities was meant

to instill in me—and did, but also didn't),
stayed on for hours one day after a moment

of kindness from you that took me by surprise.
You make me want to do likewise

for you (and OK, for others, but including the part
about being taken off guard).

Of course, none of this
is what we laugh about or discuss.

Nor, for instance, do I say
that the fact you never photograph or display

your fine collage work must derive
from your undistinguished but competitive

mother, that you're not free
(and thank you, Mom of M.). You don't tell me

that I remain afraid of
my own mother's chilled, quicksilver "love,"

scared of her every move, slow
or darting; that I'm not free. With the proviso,

though, that such meta-conversations
might sometimes be more useful than

the etiquette of silence, the right to say
almost anything stays

reserved on both sides, the bits
of our understanding like boxed units

in a couple of warehouses—no, more
organic than that, like grain reliably stored

in silos off in the distance.
Living, we agree, in its best instances

has to do with finding out more about
how to be alive, or learning about

how better to learn—something like that.
Which is like sharing, oh, a recessive trait

evident only now and then,
mostly as an outlook, a kind of motion

of the mind, a diploidy
(or, considering other friends, a polyploidy

maybe). Now, of course, being busy,
every day world-arrangingly busy,

each in our separate regions,
we see to it we don't meet often.

"Falling in love," then, cannot happen.
What we won't do, in any version of heaven,

is fall in love, O Tough and Steady, Middlesweet,
O Worker Bee—none of that

dream-pervaded, high-strung
passivity permitted to the old and to the young.

This One

For Jeredith

How did it happen, this
unlikeliness?

An emphasis
in your past, was it, or mine, so a crisis

was step-asideable? What criss-
crossed, considering the rigor mortis

of my adolescence and the non-bliss
of yours, followed by labored learning's slow osmosis

for two decades after that? The x-axis
dots somehow met the axis

of y, with the current bright result. And I know this
much: it's all "huh?" and "whatsis?"

to me. You say you dunno, either. Genesis,
meanwhile, is

all that anyone longs to know about: the first basis
of the body, of those parents over there, of this

sphere in space, or anything that is
changing, such as, oh, the Coriolis

effect on the breeze, or a shift in stasis
so feeling can begin, including this

one, emphatic as clematis
rickracking now across the backyard trellis.

A quick crushing: is
that what the facts are doing? Re-synthesis

in a micro-moment as the past compresses
into the one fat dot of "This Is

It"? So a back-of-the-neck kiss
and a bronze recovered below the Acropolis

instantly connect to the Lewis
and Clark expedition, the total Kiwanis

membership, and a recipe with orris?
Eventually, since my secret name was Limnanthis

(in my twenties) and since you like waffles, is
it certain we'd happen, without work or promises?

Sailing to Mytilene

To a young woman at a bus stop in San Francisco
and for anyone young and lonely

It's not as if I don't remember
that concentration, the fever

of waiting, alert for a sign
that the world (with all its confines

and premises, any of which,
it seems, could be erased or switched),

might actually
have moments of less difficulty

and unease. There's a tautness
in you, a fine almost-overwroughtness,

listening to everything . . .
Your eyelashes are another small, stringed

instrument. You are a bright conclusion,
what the world in any of its persuasions

calls beautiful. And the waves
of traffic past this broken-paved,

crowded, bus-stop corner
are racketing with a purpose to more

than—what?, a thousand destinations
per hour?—Mytilene only one

among them. We stand apart.
I won't see you again, we aren't

likely to speak. But, maybe
because your hopes are so solitary,

so much at risk for self-despair,
I find I've a wish for you. I'm sure

no one has pronounced it, ever,
on your behalf, and it's one I'd offer

as unpresumingly as possible, just for
your inner ear. It's a wish for

luck, of course, but only of a certain
kind, not the poses and protestations

you're all too likely to find
the sea of the real world delivering, end-over-end

into your life. Those wastes: the pouts
and sullenness of "love" that then turns out

to lack an empathy and deep world-interest
while keeping a fierce agenda about its past;

also, the drunk or clenched or over-layered,
the sexual wanderers

and the sexual frantics. Or the blur,
awful, after small but elongated failures

of sincerity, when feelings have been
explained too little or too much. Or the line,

fraying, with which you'd anchored
—feeling incandescent, delivered—

in someone who then becomes
half-hearted, unconvinced. Or some

other— Well, but what do you really
want, I wonder?, vagrantly

young, whom I imagine I know about.
You look inward, then out

and down the street, you both notice me
and don't, a fact my vanity

registers as good and bad.
And as one who'd be glad

for a brace against vanity's maraudings,
what I wish for you is something

altogether else: the lover who is not
your heart's desire, not

your type, you think, who instead
is almost uninterestingly good

for you—something like, say, piscine
vegetables. Someone, I mean,

with whom the imagination,
always a slave at the oars, awash again

with self-dislike and rancors,
can find enough scope for

the daily, large and tiny
efforts at restraint and loyalty.

I know if you're extra-fortunate,
that lover's traits will duplicate

what I found in my own. She's clumsy at
times, aggravating, not

always endearing, a strange thing,
but her gestures are something

that skims and elegantly bends
above the long depths of her mind.

Once, in closeness,
she asked aloud—she is that generous—

"How much would I give to be
here?," and has described my body

as "those serious and glamorous depths."
Braver than I, deft,

she's another knowledgeable reptile,
able to interfere with certain of my perils,

with one or two of my undoings.
So my wish is not for vanity's dreaming

imagery, a best-that-turns-into-the-worst,
but the awkward, reversed,

and harder dream, the one so desperately
at odds with your fantasies;

may it arrive, as it usually does,
like a simple packet boat you somehow recognize.

Possibly lost, desirable: that I won't know
what becomes of you, that you won't know

that we have met—well,
there's a decorousness to that, I suppose, a still

surface I would not disturb,
just ripple lightly on this momentary curb

with a story, something you make me
think of, from Thucydides.

The Athenians, fifth century B.C.,
exultant after a long-embattled victory

over one of their most stubborn
and unruly colonies in the Aegean,

sent off a full-geared warship—late
in the day this was, after detailed debate—

back to the defeated island
to carry out their sentence and command:

that every citizen of its capital,
Mytilene, be put to death. Full

of misgivings through the night,
next morning they reopened their debate,

argued until afternoon, re-voted, and dispatched
a second ship to try to catch

the first before it put to shore,
to rescind the execution order.

Under this sky like the blue of waves,
for you as well, may you have

swift winds: the trireme
of self-hatred, sleek and trimmed

and low in the gorgeous water,
may it be overtaken by the faster

ship of mercy. Or, leaping from the anchor
like the Greeks, race from the harbor

to the assembly in the square
—where swords already glint, lifted in the air—

in time to save the old, decayed,
impoverished, noble city. And may

you find, still breathing
under the conquered walls, something worth saving.

Notes

"She Was"
One method, a slow one, for finding your way out of a maze is to touch the right or left wall, then follow that surface forward until it leads you out.

"Jeredith"
A low-pressure system rotating counterclockwise near the Earth's surface is associated with good weather.

"Sailing to Mytilene"
Also spelled Mitylene. Capital city of the island of Lesbos.

trireme: a thin, efficient, two-masted warship manned by one to four tiers of oarsmen and fronted with threatening eyes painted on the bow. A large number were launched during the devastating wars between Athens and Sparta, one episode of which involved the Athenian victory at Lesbos.

For the story of the near-destruction of Mytilene, see Book III, sections 3.35-49, The Peloponnesian War, in *The Landmark Thucydides,* Robert B. Strassler, ed. (New York: The Free Press, 1996).

Acknowledgments

Grateful acknowledgment is made to journals in which these poems first appeared, often in earlier versions:

Ellipsis "Sometimes in One's Twenties" (as: "Coasting")

The Gay & Lesbian Review "The Only Thing," "Riddle"

The Kenyon Review Mexican Morning

Big City Lit "Riddle," "Logic at Seventeen"

Rhino "Logic at Seventeen"

Sinister Wisdom "Sailing to Mytilene," "What to Wear"

"This One" is included in *Science And* (FutureCycle Press, 2014), and reprinted in *The Blue Man: Poems of the Ordinary* (FutureCycle Press, 2017).

As part of a full-length collection, *Riddle* was a finalist for the 2013 Arktoi Books poetry contest, and a finalist for the 2014 Kore Press competition.

"Sailing to Mytilene" was nominated for the 2015 Pushcart Prize.

I would like to thank Risa Denenberg, Mary Meriam and others at Headmistress Press for their confidence in this project and fine production work. A special acknowledgment is due to my spouse, the poet and critic Jeredith Merrin, who made most of the visible and invisible conditions for this book possible and who critiqued uncounted versions of each poem. My gratitude as well to Elizabeth Brown Lockman, whose editorial outlook, for many years, has been invaluable.

Headmistress Press Books

Lovely - Lesléa Newman
Teeth & Teeth - Robin Reagler
How Distant the City - Freesia McKee
Shopgirls - Marissa Higgins
Riddle - Diane Fortney
When She Woke She Was an Open Field - Hilary Brown
God With Us - Amy Lauren
A Crown of Violets - Renée Vivien tr. Samantha Pious
Fireworks in the Graveyard - Joy Ladin
Social Dance - Carolyn Boll
The Force of Gratitude - Janice Gould
Spine - Sarah Caulfield
Diatribe from the Library - Farrell Greenwald Brenner
Blind Girl Grunt - Constance Merritt
Acid and Tender - Jen Rouse
Beautiful Machinery - Wendy DeGroat
Odd Mercy - Gail Thomas
The Great Scissor Hunt - Jessica K. Hylton
A Bracelet of Honeybees - Lynn Strongin
Whirlwind @ Lesbos - Risa Denenberg
The Body's Alphabet - Ann Tweedy
First name Barbie last name Doll - Maureen Bocka
Heaven to Me - Abe Louise Young
Sticky - Carter Steinmann
Tiger Laughs When You Push - Ruth Lehrer
Night Ringing - Laura Foley
Paper Cranes - Dinah Dietrich
On Loving a Saudi Girl - Carina Yun
The Burn Poems - Lynn Strongin
I Carry My Mother - Lesléa Newman
Distant Music - Joan Annsfire
The Awful Suicidal Swans - Flower Conroy
Joy Street - Laura Foley
Chiaroscuro Kisses - G.L. Morrison
The Lillian Trilogy - Mary Meriam
Lady of the Moon - Amy Lowell, Lillian Faderman, Mary Meriam
Irresistible Sonnets - ed. Mary Meriam
Lavender Review - ed. Mary Meriam

www.ingramcontent.com/pod-product-compliance
Lightning Source LLC
Chambersburg PA
CBHW070458050426
42449CB00012B/3032